THE
DUCT
TAPE
BOOK

by Tim and Tim

Pfeifer-Hamilton
Duluth, Minnesota

Pfeifer-Hamilton Publishers
210 West Michigan
Duluth MN 55802-1908   218-727-0500

The Duct Tape Book

Printed in the United States of America by Lithocolor Press, Inc.
15   14   13

Manuscript Editor: Tony Dierckins

Text: Jim Berg and Tim Nyberg
Illustrations: Tim Nyberg

Library of Congress Cataloging in Publication Data
94-22758

ISBN 1-57025-042-1

Special thanks to Julie, Kelly, Gloria, Vickie, Sherrie, Belgie, Jake, Jana, Emiah, Sam, Isaac, Jordan, Dana, Lauren, Rachel, and Lukas, who all offered creative uses for the wonder tape, and to Grandpa Bill who inspired humor in all of us. Thanks to Dot, Rob, Marina, and Julie for proofing this hodge-podge.

FOREWORD

We bet you have your own favorite uses for duct tape. This special adhesive may be holding down an unruly corner of your carpet. It's probably stopping a leak in your neighbor's hose. It may be keeping the stuffing inside grandpa's favorite chair. It is—believe it or not—sealing the seams in your furnace duct work.

Like many other duct tape enthusiasts, you may be unaware of its original function. Experts speculate a frustrated heating engineer invented duct tape while searching for a durable way to eliminate air leaks in duct work. The result? A strong adhesive applied to a cloth-reinforced base with a matte gray metallic finish to match sheet metal ducts—an ingeniously-simple miracle tape that helps air circulate throughout your home.

We, like you, thought we knew all there was to know about duct tape. Then we met Jim and Tim. On the surface, these two guys—like duct tape—seem simple. But their insights and observations have forged one of the most important home reference manuals we've seen in years. We hope it enhances your future taping experiences.

–The Editor

A DISCLAIMER BY THE AUTHORS:

This book contains humor. Please don't try any of the hints that seem blatantly stupid, potentially injurious, disrespectful to human and/or animal life, or outright dangerous. Some of the hints are real, but most are merely for your entertainment (that is, of course, assuming you find extreme stupidity entertaining). If you would like to share with us your own weird uses of duct tape, we just might include them in a future book. Send them to us in care of the publisher or via the information superhighway at Internet address: ducttape2@aol.com Remember to include your name, city, and state so we can give you proper credit. Enjoy the book and happy taping!

— Jim & Tim

Hate finding your mailbox clogged with junk mail, advertising circulars, and bills? Duct tape your mailbox shut. **1**

Stop the onslaught of junk mail with just two strips!

Obliterate that blinking "12:00" on your VCR once and for all with a single strip of duct tape. **2**

3 Lower a receding hairline:
Stretch duct tape from forehead to chin
and then open mouth. Or, for a less
radical approach, make big, tall
eyebrows of duct tape to give
the illusion of a lower hairline.

Gals—duct tape keeps the toilet seat down. **4**

Guys—duct tape keeps the toilet seat up. **5**

6 Make instant snow pants:
Cover the kids' old jeans from ankle to waist with duct tape.

7 Wrap sticky-side out around your hand to pick up fuzz, lint,
and pet hair from clothing and furniture—also picks up
small pets from clothing and furniture.

Reinforce broken candles with the silver-gray wonder roll. **8**
Adds a special aroma when the candles burn
down to the tape. Empty duct tape rolls
also make decorative holders
for extra-fat candles.

*Beautifully restore
your broken candles.*

9   Who needs a professional framer? Quickly mat your favorite art or secure photos in frame behind existing matting. California residents: tired of straightening framed pictures after every little aftershock? Secure with duct tape!

Save money with silvery-gray matting material on a roll.

Replace winter boots with socks wrapped **10**
in several layers of duct tape.

Tape hand-held games to your car's steering wheel for **11**
amusement during afternoon traffic jams.
Also great on trips!*

Not recommended by Ralph Nader or the National Safety Council.

12 Stop tables from wobbling with a wad of duct tape under the short leg. Duct tape under the bottom of all four legs provides a uniform look while preventing floor scratching.

13 High chair falling apart after the third kid? Duct tape will make it last for three or four more. You may also want to tape your kid to the seat to avoid mid-meal slippage.

Wrap silvery duct tape around cardboard shapes to create **14** prop knives and swords for your community theatre. Also holds scenery in place.

Bring your production of Macbeth to life as your local Elizabethans stab each other with realistic—but safe— duct tape prop knives.

15 Make a fashion statement:
Patch old blue jeans
with duct tape.

*Reinforce the knees
of your jeans with a
quick wrap.*

Broken wooden serving spoons? **16**
Repair with duct tape—instant mock-silver service.

Stop those embarrassing perspiration stains on shirts **17**
with a slab of tape in each armpit.

18 Reinforce Dad's old wallet—
bulging not from cash, but from his
vast collection of credit cards.

19 Detain captured burglars:
What's the next step after conking an intruder on the head
with a frying pan? Wrap perpetrator head to toe with
duct tape, call 911, and wait for the authorities.

Has dolly lost its head?
Reattach with duct tape and dolly gets a new space-age turtle neck. Or use duct tape to create a complete hi-tech ensemble.

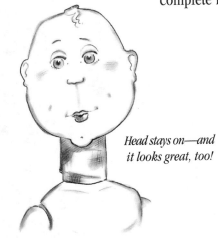

Head stays on—and it looks great, too!

21 Tired of refrigerator magnets tumbling to the floor each
time you reach for a cold drink?
Duct tape will hold the kids'
artwork until they graduate.

*Won't fall off
when door opens.*

Cover all new furniture with duct tape to **22**
keep it clean and prevent wear.

Tape furnace ductwork.* **23**

*We have never actually tried this one and have no idea if it works.
Therefore, we can only suggest this use, not actually recommend it.*

24 Quiet noisy kids:
Make a Wacky-Roller™ duct tape ball to keep them busy.
If all else fails, simply tape their mouths shut.

25 Why spend the money for press-on fingernails?
Fake fingernails made of duct tape take any polish,
and the natural gray color of duct tape nails has universal
appeal. Or, if you like the natural look, duct tape quickly
removes nail polish with just one yank!

Bind your submarine sandwich for intact transportation. **26**

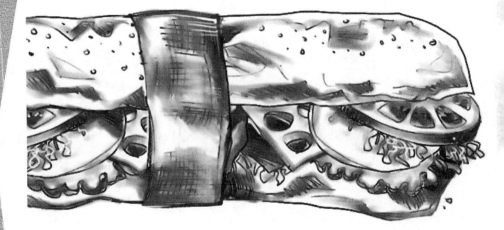

27 Save your instep!
Create a cushioned arch for your shoes
with duct tape and cotton balls.

*Cut-away illustration shows
cotton-ball-and-duct-tape
arch support enhancer.*

Remove roadkill while keeping your hands clean. **28**

Use man's best friend (duct tape) to make a nifty collar **29**
for man's other best friend—a great heavy-metal
look for your pit bull wannabe.

30 Fido sank his teeth into the kids' favorite ball? Repair it with duct tape by covering the holes with clever cut-outs.

31 Add new life to your library: Frayed and broken book spines look new after applying duct tape. Create a matching bookmark by simply folding over a strip of duct tape (particularly appropriate for reading this very book).

33 Repair and enhance sporting goods: Use duct tape as an inexpensive alternative for regripping golf clubs, to repair splitting handles on ping pong paddles, and as a grip enhancer for baseball bats and hockey sticks. It's also great for marking driveway basketball courts or for repairing worn lines on ping pong and foosball tables. Broken golf clubs? Create a duct tape handle on shortened staffs for the kids.

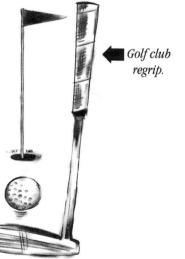

Golf club regrip.

THE DUCT TAPE BOOK

Your spouse's "troubled" aunt stopping over for a visit? **34**
Control her with a duct tape strait jacket.

Use duct tape to create a wallpaper border **35**
around your workshop.

36 Plumbing problems?
Sometimes it'll take a whole roll to stop a pesky leak,
but heck, it's still cheaper than a plumber.

37 Go for that scholarly look by taping elbow patches
on your sport coat.

DUCT TAPE AND THE AUTOMOBILE

Don't leave your driveway without a roll in the trunk, glove compartment, or right over the stick shift for convenience sake. Almost everyone has used duct tape to patch mufflers and tail pipes or to fix broken radiator hoses. The following three pages outline just some of the many other things duct tape can do for you on the road.

SUPER BONUS SECTION #1

■ Auto body repair in a roll—covered rust goes into remission. Why not cover your entire car to rustproof it? You'll never have to wax again!

■ The kids' vinyl car seats can crack in the cold. Duct tape withstands the pressures of cold weather and wiggly bottoms.

■ Loose mounting brackets or unsightly rust? Go to the roll for auto bumper repair.

■ Your quarter panel decided to leave the car and drag on your tire? Duct tape it in place before you have to replace the tire.

■ Holds translucent red plastic over broken taillight.

SUPER BONUS SECTION #1

■ A duct tape center spool taped to your dashboard makes a fine beverage can holder. Cut a notch in the side to accommodate the handle of your favorite coffee cup.

■ Replace broken antenna with duct tape and a wire coat hanger.

■ Tape garage door opener to visor.

■ Tire repair (multiple layers may be required).

■ Tow cars with several layers of duct tape in long strips.

SUPER BONUS SECTION #1

■ Mock Landau roof.

■ Mock Landau roof repair.

■ Seal cracks in dashboard—or use to decorate.

■ Increase winter warmth by taping cardboard in front of car radiator.

■ With duct tape, who needs luggage racks? Simply duct tape your luggage to the top of your car.

■ Replace missing spots on fuzzy dice with duct tape dots. Better yet, replace your fuzzy dice with a duct tape ball.

Waterproof shoes and boots by covering them entirely in duct tape. **38**

Hold great grandpa upright in his chair.* **39**

* This hint not endorsed by AARP.

THE DUCT TAPE BOOK

40 Cut costs on cosmetic surgery: Tape from chin, over forehead, to back of neck for an instant chin lift. Hide duct tape under wig.

Toupee covers tape

Notice dramatic change in user's profile.

Stop eyeglasses from slipping down your nose **41**
by taping them to your face.

Clothe naked statuary. **42**

43 Repair eyeglass bows for that classic nerd-look.
Star Trek fan? Make space-age eyewear by covering all but
a narrow slit in the lens of your eyeglasses.

44 Save money on haircuts—simply press tape onto hair and
pull very quickly. For a neater trim, pull up slowly while
clipping underlying hair with tin snips or hacksaw blade.

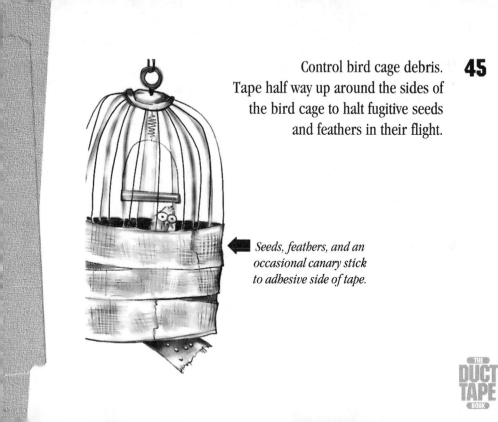

Control bird cage debris.
Tape half way up around the sides of
the bird cage to halt fugitive seeds
and feathers in their flight.

*Seeds, feathers, and an
occasional canary stick
to adhesive side of tape.*

THE
DUCT
TAPE
BOOK

46 Retail employees and waitpersons: Don't feel like smiling? Stretch duct tape from each side of mouth around to the back of your head for a perma-smile.
(We think this hint is being successfully implemented by some televangelists.)

Gold tooth optional.

Avoid dangerous jewelry pins by creating your own faux **47**
silver accessories with duct tape. Sticks to lapels,
ties, and earlobes with ease.

Lift and separate. **48**

49 Reinforce window panes and secure household items in preparation for hurricanes.
Better yet, wrap up the whole house.

50 Keep socks from falling down.

*Caution:
may remove leg hair.*

*Swim, ski, wrestle, bungee
jump, and parachute with
confidence after securing
your hair piece with
duct tape.*

THE
DUCT
TAPE
BOOK

52 Shingle your bird houses with duct tape—the silvery color reflects the heat of summer providing cooling that your feathered friends will truly appreciate.

Duct tape milk cartons together for a **53** sturdy yet inexpensive raft.

Label anything—even the kids. **54** You only need duct tape and a waterproof marker.

55 Ensure safety at kids' parties:
Replace dangerous tacks by playing "Duct Tape the Tail On the Donkey." Also makes wonderful blindfolds for "Duct Tape the Tail" and piñata action. Or give each child a strip or two for a spirited game of "Where Will the Duct Tape Stick?"

56 Guard tender bottoms from slivers in wooden swing seats, lawn furniture, and outhouse seats.
Also makes a great sliver remover.
Simply tape and yank!

Nothing says "keep out" like a few well-placed strips of duct tape.

*Not currently endorsed by ASPCA.

58 Fool your friends!
Divert them with roadrunner/coyote
phoney center lines.*

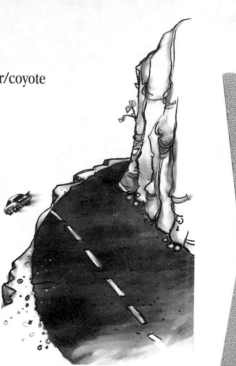

*Not recommended by the
National Safety Council,
but highly utilized by the
National Guild of Animators.*

Line bottoms of paper plates to prevent Jello™ **59**
and baked bean melt-through.

Reinforce toe shoes for heavy metal ballets. **60**

61 Bind printed reports—especially appropriate for the construction industry.

62 Sagging draperies?
Duct tape repairs curtain rods and provides lift-assist.
Also makes wonderful draping tiebacks.

Keep beverages cold for hours with just a few layers of tape and some newspaper.

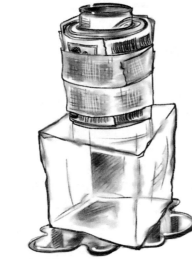

Ice also aids in keeping beverages cold for hours, though not actually part of hint #63.

DUCT TAPE AND ELECTRICITY

Duct tape can help maintain electric appliances around the house, but be careful: some brands of duct tape contain aluminum and can act as a conductor. Really. We checked. So before you try some of the hints below, call a professional— especially if you don't know the first thing about dealing with electricity. We don't either.

■ Organize audio/video cable and unused extension cords by taping the unwieldy snakes together.

■ Hold wires in place while soldering.

■ Save on energy costs: tape over switches to be kept in the "off" position.

SUPER BONUS SECTION #2

■ Tape television and VCR remote controls to couch arm to prevent loss.

■ Secure loose speakers to your boombox.

■ Keep counter-top appliance cords neatly in place behind appliances. Also keep vibrating appliances in place and on the counter.

Duct tape also covers those scratchy little nubbies on Grandma's couch.

64 Increase your on-base percentage: Distract pitchers by taping small sculptures to your batting helmet. ("Ball four, take your base. . . .")

Patch aluminum siding, then just spray paint to match **65**
the house. Still painting every other year?
Avoid pushy aluminum siding
salespeople by simply taping
your entire house.

Who needs to know how to sew? **66**
Duct tape hems pants and
skirts in a jiffy!

67 Need a temporary wedding band?
Hey, what the heck, with a product this
durable—make a permanent wedding band!

68 Compulsive lawn mowers and snow shovelers:
Enjoy worry-free breaks by using duct tape to mark
where you leave off. Also creates a non-stick
surface for snow shovels.

Waterproof your camera: **69**
Just tape it into a plastic
bag for in-the-rain and
underwater shots.

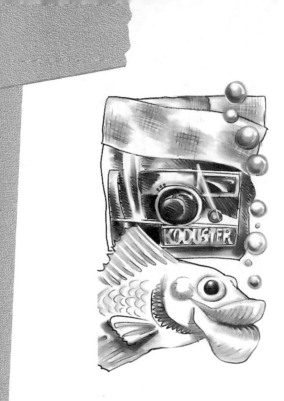

70   Small towns:
Easily change your population signs
with duct tape and a marker.

*Not really, we just like to sound like big important
guys once in a while. Play along with us.*

73   Lost in the woods?
Not with duct tape around! Just hang little strips
of tape from branches to find your way back.

74   Remodelling on a budget?
Cover cupboard doors and drawer fronts for a modern,
metallic-look kitchen.

Combine burger flipper and a fly swatter for convenient cookout insect control.

Fly shown not actual size.

76 Wrap a brick for an effective
and decorative doorstop.
Better yet, duct tape the door open!

Instant swimsuit. (To avoid embarrassing nudity, **77**
do not apply when wet.)

Super-seal your tax return envelope to annoy the IRS. **78**
And when you've finished your taxes, patch the
fist hole in your wall with duct tape.

79 First on the scene of a major accident?
Combine duct tape with blankets for instant massive
bandages. You can also use duct tape and
two-by-fours for emergency splints.

80 Look like a professional musician:
Duct tape makes a great guitar case reinforcer and
a lovely companion to Grateful Dead stickers.

Taxi drivers: Sandwich marbles between two layers of duct tape for a do-it-yourself beaded car seat.

This marks the halfway point of The Duct Tape Book. *We hope you are enjoying the wealth of usable information that we have assembled as much as Alma Jacobson did:*

"I can't begin to express my appreciation for your hard work in assembling, in one easy reference manual, all of this useful duct tape information. I am running out right now to pick up extra copies for my niece, who is getting married, my neighborhood handyman, and my son's home reference library."

–Alma Jacobson

Thanks Alma! –The Authors

---

82 Renew torn window shades.
Heck, tape up the whole
window for perma-shade!

Prevent oil stains by covering the entire garage floor with duct tape—provides a shiny new finish, too! **83**

Patch hot air balloons.* **84**

Use at your own risk.

85   Add a personal touch to gifts:
Nothing says "I care" better than a gift wrapped entirely in
duct tape (the reusable wrapping paper).

86   Neighbor kid wrecked your favorite tree?
Splint broken limbs with a few sticks and some duct tape.
You can also create everlasting leaf replacements by folding
duct tape in half, cutting leaf shapes, adhering to a wire
coat hanger, and spraying with green enamel paint.

Attach decoys around bird bath to welcome strangers.

Realistic decoy attracts birds.

Also patches holes!

THE DUCT TAPE BOOK

88 Telemarketers: Tape phone to head to relieve crick in neck. Folks annoyed by telemarketers: Tape over phone earpiece to relieve pain in neck.

Cover barbs on barbed wire for safety. **89**

Hang a strip from the ceiling—instant fly trap. **90**

91 Enjoy your music loud?
Tape volume knob at your favorite level. Tape vibrating
stereo to table. Tape vibrating table to floor.
In most cases, foundation should
secure floor.

92 Cover nasty pet stains in carpets. Better yet, cover entire
carpet while potty training puppies. Simply peel away
once the dog has learned to scratch at the door.
By the way, a strip or two on the door prevents
dog's scratching from marring wood.

Fasten equipment inside jacket while on secret spy missions.

Always carry a few extra strips of duct tape, too.

94   Display your concern for animal welfare:
Tape turtles shell to shell so if they accidentally get turned
over, they can still get where they're going.

Mute guitars by taping over the sound hole. **95**
While you're at it, mute lousy singers
by taping over their sound hole.

Muzzle your mutt!* **96**

*You may need to tape a straw in dog's mouth to allow
for drinking on hot days. This hint, by the way, is
also not currently endorsed by anybody.*

97 Teach kids about safety by using duct tape to make seat belts for their dolls. Also keeps pets in place.

98 Call it gaff tape and use it to hold wires, lighting equipment, etc., in place on stages and movie sets.*

*Again, we have never actually tried this and can only speculate as to its success. This is only a suggestion, not a recommendation.

Expedite exit from airports: **99**
A big **X** on your suitcase makes
locating it at the baggage
claim carousel a snap.

◀ *Just spot the duct tape* **X**
and you're on your way!

THE DUCT TAPE BOOK

100 Simulate a surprised look—just attach duct tape from your eyebrows to the back of your head. Works best when bald.

Wrap tape around a crayon stub and cut into minnow shapes—instant fishing lures without the smell of live bait.* **1001**

Mosquito-proof your clothes—stop the little "suckers" with inpenetrable duct tape! **102**

This is really only hint #101—we just wanted to see what the book would look like if we had come up with over 1,000 hints.

103 Eliminate dangerous sharp tips of bungee cord hooks with a protective coating of duct tape.
Better yet, eliminate the need of bungee cords:
use duct tape.

104 Whoops! Got carried away jammin' and ripped your snare drum head? Duct tape to the rescue! It also dampens the sound nicely. Add depth to your rhythm section by taping pie tins together for the Caribbean sounds of mini steel drums, or duct tape the lid to a pair of empty oatmeal boxes for a set of kiddie bongos (also makes nice strap for around neck).

106 Cover your exposed skin with duct tape for a sunblock that allows you to stay out in the sun for days without burning. Going for that freckled-face look of youth? Simply punch holes in duct tape and apply to face. Too late for protection? Duct tape removes peeling, sunburned skin in a snap.

Look and feel younger after just one afternoon in the sun with duct tape screened freckles!

Stretch duct tape across the top of baby's crib for a **107** webbing that keeps baby in place.

Combine pen and pencil, writing-ends opposite, to **108** create a unique and handy pen and pencil set.

DUCT TAPING THROUGH THE HOLIDAYS

Faced with the pressures of gift buying, entertaining, and visits from the relatives? Keep a roll on hand and use some of the following hints to cut costs and reduce holiday stress:

■ Use duct tape as an Easter egg dye stencil. Better yet, why not just decorate the eggs with duct tape and avoid all the mess?

■ Hang Christmas cards on the walls or stockings over your fireplace by fastening a long strip of duct tape sticky side out.

■ Secure Christmas lights to railings.
Also secure railings to house.

■ Shred duct tape for Christmas tree tinsel.

■ Pick up fallen Christmas tree needles.

■ Cut into star shapes to mend Christmas stocking holes. Hey, why not stuff someone's stocking with a roll of duct tape? And while you're at it, stuff someone's stocking with *The Duct Tape Book*.

■ Make a metallic mummy for your haunted house next Halloween. Combine with metal funnel and dryer tubing for realistic Tinman costume (or try an astronaut or robot). Or, make a mask out of duct tape and go as every kid's favorite superhero: Duct Tape Man! Also makes great Ironman or Gladiator bracelets.

It may take a roll or two, but your haunted house will be a success with a shiny, metallic mummy!

109 Why spend the money on bikini wax?
Duct tape makes a great depilatory! It also works wonders removing nose hair, plucking eyebrows, and eliminating unsightly toe hair. Or simply cover toes to hide the hair and make a fashion statement.

110 Frayed or missing shoelace tips?
Just a mini-strip around the loose ends makes lacing easy.

Hold eyes open during your boss's boring speeches. **111**

112 Fold tape over edge of any material and
punch through for insty-grommet.

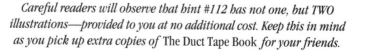

*Hang anything on pegboard
with a duct tape tab.*

*Fold over and punch
through for grommet.*

*Careful readers will observe that hint #112 has not one, but TWO
illustrations—provided to you at no additional cost. Keep this in mind
as you pick up extra copies of* The Duct Tape Book *for your friends.*

Remove dust balls under beds using these three steps: **113**
1. Wrap duct tape sticky-side out around small dog.
2. Roll the dog's favorite ball under the bed.
3. Yell "fetch!"

Pick up spilled kitty litter. **114**
Also pick up kitty.*

*Also not endorsed by the ASPCA. In fact, neither of the
hints on this page are endorsed by the ASPCA.*

115 Prevent saddle sores:
Just tape an eight-inch thick foam pad on your bike seat.

116 Bundle old magazines for recycling.
Eventually you can even build a garage
out of bundled magazines.

Hang paint brushes by handle in thinner to avoid bending bristles. Really.

 Suspend brush so bristles do not touch bottom of can.

118 Protect tip of tongue so you *can* lick cold flag poles in the winter without risk.

Stop annoying drips during the cold and flu season with a **119**
strip under the nose to block each nostril.

Naugahyde savior. **120**

121 Hold broken coffee cup handles in place while gluing. Leave duct tape on after glue sets to help identify your cup at the office.

122 Change the color of last year's ski jacket with just one roll of duct tape.

THE
DUCT
TAPE
BOOK

Hold ponytails in place or use as a headband. **123**
Caution: Coat hair with a lightweight
motor oil—we recommend 10W-30—
to prevent hair loss upon removal.

TAPE LIKE A PRO!

Use the lines on these pages to practice your taping technique. If tape doesn't make that *Err Err Err Err Screech Err Err Err* sound as you pull the duct tape off the roll, make sure you are using authentic duct tape. If you are indeed using DUCT TAPE (silvery-gray in color with a fabric-like pattern running through it), but still encounter problems, call a certified "User" to serve as your personal instructor.

– –

(Make sure it's straight!)

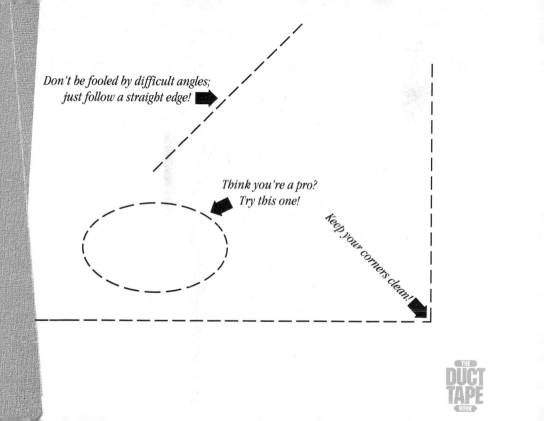

Don't be fooled by difficult angles; just follow a straight edge!

Think you're a pro? Try this one!

keep your corners clean!

124 Affix necklace clasp to the back of the neck with a two-inch slab of duct tape so clasp doesn't slide around to the front. Wad duct tape over old earrings to complete this fashion statement.

Dangling duct tape "ball" earrings accent necklace-securing strip. ➡

Prevent the accumulation of junk by taping **125**
over the top of your junk drawer.

Patch your sump pump hose.* **126**

*Of course, duct tape will fix leaks in any type of hosing.
We just like to say "sump pump."*

127 Convert sharp knives into butter knives by covering the sharp edge with duct tape.

128 Catch fly balls with the greatest of ease after covering your baseball glove pocket with duct tape, sticky side out. Also works for the hands of football receivers.

Duct tape this page with backwards type
to a wall opposite a mirror
so you can read it
more easily.

130 Cat underfoot?
Tape it to the ceiling.

Dog underfoot? **131**
Tape it to the ceiling.

Kids underfoot? **132**

133 Athletes: Tape ankles and wrists to avoid sprains and other injuries. If it's too late, tape ice bag to wounded extremities to ease pain of sprains and other injuries.

134 Affix shampoo bottle upside down on shower wall for a neat dispenser.

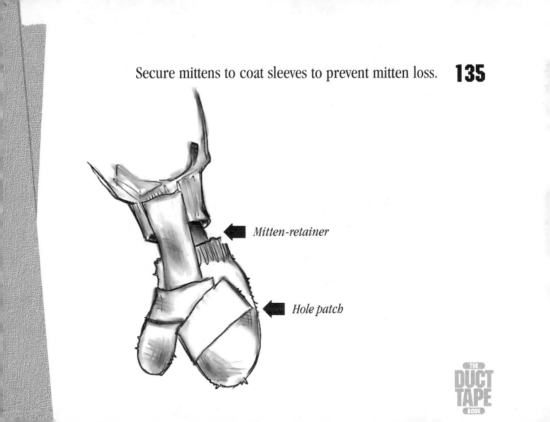

Mitten-retainer

Hole patch

THE DUCT TAPE BOOK

136 Fill unsightly tooth gaps by expanding surrounding tooth surfaces with duct tape. It'll also look like you have very expensive teeth.

Avoid annoying slippage by taping shoulder **137**
pads and bra straps in place.

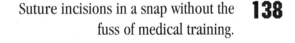

Suture incisions in a snap without the **138**
fuss of medical training.

*Insty-suture for those
do-it-yourself surgeries.*

A DUCT TAPE TIME OUT: THE GUEST PEN

Hey, Jim and me, we're getting tired of thinking.

Yeah. My head hurts, Tim.

Maybe you got your duct tape headband too tight again, Jim.

I've got an idea, Tim . . . let's introduce our special guest.

Good idea, Jim. O.K. Here's our special guest, Tony the editor guy, with a duct tape editorial-essay thing he wrote:

DUCT TAPE IN THE U.S.A. by Tony

Many Americans take duct tape—like our freedom of speech—for granted. They don't realize the important role duct tape plays in our daily lives. We absolutely depend on it. Duct tape helps bind our nation together. The quality of life we Americans enjoy would be diminished without it.

Duct tape is such an integral part of America that it has become a staple in two uniquely American art forms: motion pictures and rock and roll. The film industry uses black duct tape (called gaff tape) to secure cables and lighting instruments. On each movie set one person is charged with duct taping everything that shouldn't move, and the name of that person—the

Gaffer—appears in the credits of every movie, usually some place after the Best Boy (but before the Key Grip). The success of duct tape on movie sets quickly spread to the rock and roll stage. Today, no roadies worth their salt would work without a roll strapped to their belts, ready to hold down speaker cable and drum kit hardware.

Because of its continued use as a heating duct sealant, duct tape now surrounds us. Time and exposure to high temperatures slowly breaks duct tape down, and tiny particles drift into ducts where they are eventually carried into the air. And so duct tape is like God. It's everywhere.

On the surface, duct tape is just a handy adhesive. Deep down it is much more than that. It's the movies; it's rock and roll. It's about being part of the greatest nation on earth. And it shares a characteristic with God. No, duct tape is not just about sticking things together. It's about God and Country. Use it and be proud.

Hey, Tim, my head hurts worse now.

Yeah. That's a lot to think about. But then, duct tape is worthy of such high-quality thought. . . . We better get back to the book. Take an aspirin, Jim.

I've got two duct taped to my leg, Tim.

Hey, another hint, Jim.

Yeah.

139 Remove shell bits from hard-boiled eggs—
just dab sticky side on shell fragments.

140 Join two pets, tail to tail, and see what happens.*

*Hint #140 is also not endorsed by anyone that we know, although it would be kind of fun to watch, wouldn't it?

Secure lid to outdoor cooker for a mess-free transport to tailgate parties or after a successful afternoon of trapping small woodland creatures.

Keeps coals, grill, and muskrat inside!

142 A major problem in the 50s and 60s that still plagues some families today is easily repaired with duct tape. Of course, we're talking about those bent and crimped metal TV tray, card table, and folding chair legs. You can also avoid accidental tippage by taping plates and utensils to TV trays in high-traffic areas.

Leg repair shown here uses a piece of 1" x 2" #2 white pine splints and duct tape.

No shoelaces? Worn-out velcro? **143**
Tape your shoes to your feet.

Repair ripped duct tape. **144**

145 Massage your feet while you walk:
Just tape olive pits to the insoles of your shoes.

146 Secure kids' stocking caps to their heads
to avoid loss while sledding.
Secure kids to sled to avoid
loss while sledding.

THE
DUCT
TAPE
BOOK

148 Trap mice the humane way—simply lay a strip of duct tape on the floor, sticky side up, like fly paper. To be extra nice, leave mice a piece of cheese to nibble while they wait to be removed.

Perma-fix holes in heels of socks. **149**
Better yet, prevent holes by
taping them right out
of the package.

Hinge-O-Matic™—duct tape makes a quick, inexpensive **150**
temporary replacement for worn or broken hinges.

151 Hold back epidermal layers during difficult surgical procedures.

152 Wind proof your picnic table cloth with a strip on each corner. Or, you might as well cover entire picnic table in duct tape for easy clean up.

Press-n-yank loose teeth from their sockets. **153**
Remember to dry tooth thoroughly before applying tape.

154 Cover birthmarks.

You can also create temporary birthmarks: simply stick tape on desired area, leave it on five to ten minutes, and then rip it off quickly.

This illustration has nothing to do with hint #154; it actually goes with hint #153. We turned it upside down to show you how to remove a tooth from the lower jaw.

Restless sleeper? Tape bed sheets in place. **155A**

Sleep Walker? Tape sleeper in place. **155B**

Achieve that Vegas-era Elvis look **156**
by taping the lapels of
an old sport coat.

← *Also makes a great cummerbund or girdle!*

157 Repair power tool housing—
keeps the inside in and the outside out.
Quite honestly, duct tape replaces most power tools.

158 Mend patio furniture:
Duct tape is less expensive and stronger than that
plastic webbing stuff they're originally made of.

Be kind to animals: **159**
Tape corncobs to trees for birds and squirrels.
Or, tape birds and squirrels to trees
for dogs and cats.*

*This hint is definitely not endorsed by
the ASPCA. In fact, Tim's wife (Jim's
sister) and Jim's wife (Tim's sister-in-
law) said we should take it out. But we
figure, hey, it's only a joke. Anyone
who would take this hint seriously
should be duct taped to the tree right
next to the squirrel.*

THE
**DUCT
TAPE**
BOOK

160 Seal packages with duct tape so even the postal service won't be able to damage the enclosed contents. Triple-taping your return merchandise also really irritates mail-order vendors.

Last illustration in the book.
(First illustration for those
who read backwards.)

RETURN T
SENDE
3702 NC
SHERM

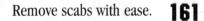

Remove scabs with ease. **161**

Write a book about duct tape's many uses. **162**

TALK LIKE A DUCT TAPE PRO!

DUCT TAPE

Not: "The [washing machine] is broken."
But: "The [washing machine] lacks duct tape."

Try to work these phrases into everyday conversations:

- D'ya duct tape that yourself?
- Duct tape changed my life.
- I'm wearing duct tape.
- Duct tape: it's not just for ducts anymore.
- Don't leave home without duct tape.
- It'd be cheaper to duct tape it.
- My name is _____ and I'm addicted to duct tape.
- If at first you don't succeed, duct tape it.
- Duct tape saved my marriage.
- Duct tape: the ultimate power tool.

READ MORE ABOUT DUCT TAPE

Although *The Duct Tape Book* is the most exhaustive reference manual ever compiled about duct tape, if you want to learn more about this subject, look for these inspiring books at your local library:

Zen and the Art of Duct Tape

Moby Duct

The Duct Tape Diet

The Tao of Duct Tape

How Duct Tape Works

Gone with the Duct Tape

The Three Duct Tapeketeers

The Duct Tape of Madison County

The One Minute Duct Taper

What Color is Your Duct Tape?

The Duct Tape in the Rye

The Taping of the Shrew

Anne of Green Duct Tape

A Wrinkle in Duct Tape

Duct Taping in America

War and Duct Tape

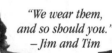